MR. SERJEANT BUZFUZ.

The Law

and

Lawyers of Pickwick.

A LECTURE.

With an Original Drawing of "Mr. Serjeant Buzfuz."

BY

FRANK LOCKWOOD,
Q.C. M.P.

SECOND EDITION.

THE LAWBOOK EXCHANGE, LTD.
Clark, New Jersey

ISBN 978-1-58477-231-6

Lawbook Exchange edition 2002, 2017

The quality of this reprint is equivalent to the quality of the original work.

THE LAWBOOK EXCHANGE, LTD.
33 Terminal Avenue
Clark, New Jersey 07066-1321

*Please see our website for a selection of our other publications
and fine facsimile reprints of classic works of legal history:*
www.lawbookexchange.com

Library of Congress Cataloging-in-Publication Data

Lockwood, Frank, Sir, 1846-1897.
   The law and lawyers of Pickwick : a lecture / by Frank Lockwood.
   p. cm.
   "With an original drawing of 'Mr. Serjeant Buzfuz.'"
   Reprint. Originally published: London: Roxburghe Press, 1894?
   ISBN 1-58477-231-X (cloth: alk. paper)
   1. Dickens, Charles, 1812-1870. Pickwick papers. 2. Dickens,
Charles, 1812-1870—Knowledge—Law. 3. Lawyers in literature. 4. Law in
literature. I. Title.

PR4569 .L6 2002
823'.8—dc21   2002024329

Printed in the United States of America on acid-free paper

The Law

and

Lawyers of Pickwick.

A LECTURE.

With an Original Drawing of "Mr. Serjeant Buzfuz."

BY

FRANK LOCKWOOD,

Q.C. M.P.

SECOND EDITION.

LONDON:

THE ROXBURGHE PRESS,

3, Victoria Street, Westminster,

AND

32, CHARING CROSS, S.W.

𝕬niform with this 𝕰bition.

CHARLES DICKENS' HEROINES AND WOMEN-FOLK :

Some Thoughts Concerning Them.

BY

CHARLES F. RIDEAL.

With an original Drawing of Edith Dombey.

PREFATORY.

A T the request of my friend
Lord Russell of Killowen, then
Attorney-General, I delivered this
lecture at the Morley Hall, Hackney,
on December 13th, 1893. I had
previously delivered it in the city of
York at the request of some of my
constituents. I feel that some apology
is required for its reproduction in a
more permanent form, which apology
I most respectfully tender to all who
may read this little book.

F. L.

THE
LAW
AND
LAWYERS
OF
PICKWICK.

THE LAW AND LAWYERS
OF " PICKWICK."

———◆———

Sir CHARLES RUSSELL : I stand but for a single instant between you and our friend, Mr. Lockwood. He needs no introduction here ; but I am sure I may in your name bid him a hearty welcome.

Mr. FRANK LOCKWOOD : Mr. Attorney-General, Ladies and Gentlemen—It is some little time ago that I was first asked whether I was prepared to deliver a lecture. Now I am bound at the outset to confess to you that lecturing has been and is very

little in my way. I spent some three
years of my life at the University
in avoiding lectures. But it came
about that in the constituency which I
have the honour to represent, it was
suggested to me that it was necessary for me to give a lecture, and
it was further explained to me that
it did not really very much matter
as to what I lectured about. I am
bound to say there was a very great
charm to me in the idea of lecturing
my constituents. I know it does
sometimes occur that constituents
lecture their representatives, especially in Scotland, and I was anxious,
if I might, to have an opportunity of
lecturing those who had so many
opportunities of reading, no doubt
very useful lectures to me. But the
difficulty was to find a subject. My
own profession suggested itself to me

as a fit topic for a lecture, but unfortunately my profession is not a popular one. I do not know how it is, but you never find a lawyer introduced either into a play or into a three-volume novel except for the purpose of exposing him as a scoundrel in the one, and having him kicked in the third act in the other. I do not know how it is, but so it is. All the heroes of fiction either in the drama or in the novel are found in the ranks—no, not in the ranks of the army, but in the officers of the army, or in the clergy. It is so in novels, it is so in dramas; Mr. Attorney-General, I believe it is so in real life.

And so, looking about for a subject, being reminded, as I was, that the subject of the law was unpopular, I turned—as I have often done in the hour of trouble—I turned to my

Dickens, and there I found that at
any rate in Dickens we have a great
literary man who has been impartial
in his treatment of lawyers. He has
seen both the good and the bad in
them, and it occurred to me that my
lecture might take the form of dealing
with the lawyers of Dickens. I soon
found that was too great a subject to
be dealt with within the short space
which could be accorded to any
reasonable lecturer by any reasonable
audience. I found that the novels of
Dickens abounded with lawyers, to
use a perhaps apt expression. Having
regard to my profession, they fairly
bristled with them, and so I determined to take the lawyers of one of
his books ; and I chose as that book
" Pickwick " ; and I chose as my title
" The Law and the Lawyers of ' Pickwick.' "

Ladies and gentlemen, it is an extraordinary thing when we look at this book, when we reflect that it contains within its pages no less than three hundred and sixty characters, all drawn vividly and sharply, all expressing different phases of human thought, and of human life, and every one of them original; when we reflect that that book was written by a young man of twenty-three years of age. In that book I found that he portrayed with life-like fidelity constables, sheriffs' officers, beadles, ushers, clerks, solicitors, barristers, and last, but by no means least, a judge. Every incident of the early life of this great author bore fruit in his writings. No portion of his struggles and experiences seemed to have made a deeper impress on him than did those early days, as he said

himself in the character of David
Copperfield :—

If it should appear from anything I may
set down in this narrative that I was a child
of close observation, or that as a man I
have a strong memory of my childhood, I
undoubtedly lay claim to both of these
characteristics.

His first introduction to the terrors
of the law was an unspeakably sad
one—sad, indeed, to his affectionate
and imaginative nature. " I know,"
he writes, " that we got on very badly
with the butcher and baker, that very
often we had not too much for dinner,
and that at last my father was
arrested." He never forgot—how
could he, knowing what we know
the lad to have been ?—often carrying
messages to the dismal Marshalsea.
" I really believed," he wrote, " that

they had broken my heart." His first
visit to his father he thus describes :—

My father was waiting for me in the
lodge, and we went up to his room (on the
top story but one), and cried very much.
And he told me, I remember, to take
warning by the Marshalsea, and to observe
that if a man had twenty pounds a year
and spent nineteen pounds nineteen shillings and sixpence, he would be happy,
but that a shilling spent the other way
would make him wretched. I see the fire
we sat before now, with two bricks inside
the rusted grate, one on each side, to
prevent its burning too many coals. Some
other debtor shared the room with him,
who came in by-and-by ; and as the dinner
was a joint stock repast I was sent up to
"Captain Porter" in the room overhead,
with Mr. Dickens's compliments, and I
was his son, and could he, Captain P., lend
me a knife and fork ?

Captain Porter lent the knife and fork,

with his compliments in return. There
was a very dirty lady in his room, and two
wan girls, his daughters, with shock heads
of hair. I thought I should not have liked
to borrow Captain Porter's comb. The
Captain himself was in the last extremity
of shabbiness ; and if I could draw at all,
I would draw an accurate portrait of the
old, old, brown great-coat he wore, with no
other coat below it. His whiskers were
large. I saw his bed rolled up in a corner ;
and what plates, and dishes, and pots he
had on a shelf; and I knew (God knows
how !) that the two girls with the shock
heads were Captain Porter's natural children, and that the dirty lady was not
married to Captain P. My timid, wondering station on his threshold was not occu-
pied more than a couple of minutes, I
daresay ; but I came down to the room
below with all this as surely in my
knowledge as the knife and fork were in
my hand.

When the stern necessities of the situation required the detention of Mr. Pickwick in the old Fleet Prison, we have produced a lifelike representation of the debtors' gaol ; and I believe that the reforms which have made such an institution a thing of the past are in a great part owing to the vivid recollection which enabled him to point to the horrors and injustice which were practised in the sacred name of law.

At the age of fifteen we find Dickens a bright, clever-looking youth in the office of Mr. Edward Blackmore, attorney-at-law in Gray's Inn, earning at first 13*s.* 6*d.* a week, afterwards advanced to 15*s.* Eighteen months' experience of this sort enabled him in the pages of Pickwick thus to describe lawyers' clerks :—

There are several grades of lawyers'

clerks. There is the articled clerk, who has paid a premium, and is an attorney in perspective, who runs a tailor's bill, receives invitations to parties, knows a family in Gower Street, and another in Tavistock Square; who goes out of town every Long Vacation to see his father, who keeps live horses innumerable; and who is, in short, the very aristocrat of clerks. There is the salaried clerk—out of door, or in door, as the case may be—who devotes the major part of his thirty shillings a week to his personal pleasure and adornment, repairs half-price to the Adelphi Theatre at least three times a week, dissipates majestically at the cider cellars afterwards, and is a dirty caricature of the fashion which expired six months ago. There is the middle-aged copying clerk, with a large family, who is always shabby, and often drunk. And there are the office lads in their first surtouts, who feel a befitting contempt for boys at day-schools; club as they go home at night for saveloys and porter ; and think there's nothing like "life."

I fancy Dickens never rose above the status of office boy, and probably as such wore his first surtout. We hear of him reporting later in the Lord Chancellor's Court, probably for some daily paper ; but beyond the exception which I shall mention presently, we have no record of his taking an active and direct part in any of those mysterious rites that go to make up our legal procedure.

Upon this question of the opportunities he had for knowing in what way a lawyer is trained, I must here acknowledge the debt of gratitude that I am under to my very good friend Mr. Henry Fielding Dickens, one of her Majesty's Counsel ; and how rejoiced, Mr. Attorney-General, would that father have been had he

been able to see the position which
his son has won for himself. He
wrote to me a long and kind letter, in
which he gave me further information
as to his father's opportunity for observing lawyers and their mode of
living, and he told me that which I
did not know before, and which I
think but few people knew before,
namely, that his father had kept a
term or two at one of the Inns of
Court. He had eaten the five or six
dinners which is part of the necessary
legal education for a barrister; and
he had suffered in consequence the
usual pangs of indigestion. But it
is not to that that I wish to allude
to-night. Dickens did that which I
venture to think but few have done;
for, giving up all idea of pursuing a
legal education, and finding that the
dinners did not agree with him, he

got back from the Inns of Court some
of the money which he had deposited
at that Inn. You are all familiar with
the process which is known as getting
butter out of a dog's mouth ; I venture
to think that that is an easy thing com-
pared with getting money back from
an Inn of Court.

But that is not all that Mr. Dickens
told me. He wrote down for me an
experience his father once had with
the family solicitor, which, I think, is
worth your hearing. "My father's
solicitor, Mr. Ouvry," he says, "was a
very well-known man, a thorough man
of the world, and one in whose breast
reposed many of the secrets of the
principal families of England. On
one occasion my father was in treaty
for a piece of land at the back of Gad's
Hill, and it was proposed that there
should be an interview with the owner,

a farmer, a very acute man of business, and a very hard nut to crack. It was arranged that the interview with him should be at Gad's Hill, and the solicitor came down for the purpose. My father and Ouvry were sitting over their wine when the old man was announced. 'We had better go in to him,' said my father. 'No, no,' said the astute lawyer. 'John,' said he, turning to the butler, 'show him into the study, and take him a bottle of the old port.' Then turning to my father, 'A glass of port will do him good ; it will soften him.' After waiting about twenty 'minutes they went into the study ; the farmer was sitting bolt upright in an arm-chair, stern and uncompromising ; the bottle of port had not been touched. Negotiations then proceeded very much in favour of the farmer, and a bargain was struck. The old man then proceeded to turn his attention to the port, and in a very few minutes he had finished the bottle."

Mr. Dickens also told me of his father's knowledge of the legal profession, and of the distinguished members of it. Though not himself, he writes, of the legal profession, my father was very fond of lawyers. He numbered among his intimate friends Lord Denman, Lord Campbell, Mr. Justice Talfourd, Chief Justice Cockburn; in fact, it is difficult to name any eminent lawyer who could not claim acquaintance, at any rate, with our great author. And he tells me, too, an anecdote relating to a distinguished lawyer of the present day — Sir Henry Hawkins. We nearly lost that great man, I think about the year 1851, on the occasion of some theatricals at Knebworth. The play was *Every Man in his Humour*, and Frank Stone, the artist, father of Mr. Marcus Stone, R.A., was allowed to play a part with a sword. (Those of you who have had any experience of theatrical matters know how dangerous it is to trust a sword to an amateur.) He came up flourishing the sword, and if Mr. Hawkins had not ducked we should have lost that eminent man ; but he did it just in time.

Before I introduce you to the types of the judge, the counsel, the solicitors, let me say something to you of the district in which lawyers live, or rather in Dickens's time lived, and still do congregate. From Gray's Inn in the north to the Temple in the south, from New Inn and Clement's Inn in the west to Barnard's Inn in the east.

I once lived myself in Clement's Inn,
and heard the chimes go, too ; and
I remember one day I sat in my
little room very near the sky (I do
not know why it is that poverty
always gets as near the sky as possible ; but I should think it is because
the general idea is that there is more
sympathy in heaven than elsewhere),
and as I sat there a knock came at
the door, and the head of the porter
of Clement's Inn presented itself to
me. It was the first of January, and
he gravely gave me an orange and a
lemon. He had a basketful on his
arm. I asked for some explanation.
The only information forthcoming
was that from time immemorial
every tenant on New Year's Day
was presented with an orange and a
lemon, and that I was expected, and
that every tenant was expected, to

give half-a-crown to the porter.
Further inquiries from the steward
gave me this explanation, that in
old days when the river was not used
merely as a sewer, the fruit was
brought up in barges and boats to
the steps from below the bridge and
carried by porters through the Inn
to Clare Market. Toll was at first
charged, and this toll was divided
among the tenants whose convenience
was interfered with; hence the old
lines beginning " Oranges and lemons
said the bells of St. Clement's." I
have often wondered whether the
rest of the old catch had reason as
well as rhyme.

Dickens loved the old Inns and
squares. Traddles lived in Gray's
Inn : Traddles who was in love with
" the dearest girl in the world ";
Tom Pinch and his sister used to

meet near the fountain in the Middle
Temple ; Sir John Chester had rooms
in Paper Buildings ; Pip lived in Gar-
den Court at the time of the collapse
of Great Expectations ; Mortimer
Lightwood and Eugene Wrayburn
had their queer domestic partnership
in the Temple. The scene of the
murderous plot in " Hunted Down "
is also laid in the Temple, " at the top
of a lonely corner house overlooking
the river," probably the end house of
King's Bench Walk. Mr. Grewgious,
Herbert Pocket, and Joe Gargery
are associated with Staple Inn and
Barnard's Inn.

Lincoln's Inn has not been forgotten ; for though Mr. Tulkinghorn
lived in the Fields, yet Serjeant
Snubbin was to be found in Lincoln's
Inn Old Square.

I never could understand why

Dickens located the Serjeant in the realms of Equity ; but what should interest us more to-night is the fact that the greater part of " Pickwick " was written in Furnival's Inn, which, as Dickens describes it, was " a shady, quiet place echoing to the footsteps of the stragglers there, and rather monotonous and gloomy on summer evenings."

But to know the Inns as Dickens knew them, let us accompany Mr. Pickwick to the Magpie and Stump in search of Mr. Lowten, Mr. Perker's clerk.

"Is Mr. Lowten here, ma'am ? " inquired Mr. Pickwick.

"Yes, he is, sir," replied the landlady. " Here, Charley, show the gentleman in to Mr. Lowten."

"The gen'lm'n can't go in just now," said a shambling pot-boy, with a red head,

" 'cos Mr. Lowten's singin' a comic song, and he'll put him out. He'll be done d'rectly, sir."

Well, you know, respectable solicitors (clerks) don't sing comic songs at public houses nowadays, but that is how Mr. Pickwick found Mr. Lowten.

" Would you like to join us ? " said Mr. Lowten, when at length he had finished his comic song and been introduced to Mr. Pickwick. And I am very glad that Mr. Pickwick did join them, as he heard something of the old Inns from old Jack Bamber.

" I have been to-night, gentlemen," said Mr. Pickwick, hoping to start a subject which all the company could take a part in discussing—" I have been to-night in a place which you all know very well, doubtless, but which I have not been in for some years, and know very little of; I mean

Gray's Inn, gentlemen.   Curious little
nooks in a great place, like London, these
old Inns are."

"By Jove ! " said the chairman, whisper-
ing across the table to Mr. Pickwick, " you
have hit upon something that one of us,
at least, would talk upon for ever.   You'll
draw old Jack Bamber out ; he was never
heard to talk about anything else but the
Inns, and he has lived alone in them till
he's half crazy."

"Aha ! " said the old man, a brief description of whose manner and appearance
concluded the last chapter, " aha ! who
was talking about the Inns ? "

"I was, sir," replied Mr. Pickwick ; "I
was observing what singular old places
they are."

" *You !* " said the old man, contemptu-
ously.   "What do *you* know of the time
when young men shut themselves up in
those lonely rooms, and read and read,
hour after hour, and night after night, till

their reason wandered beneath their mid-
night studies ; till their mental powers were
exhausted ; till morning's light brought no
freshness or health to them ; and they sank
beneath the unnatural devotion of their
youthful energies to their dry old books ?
Coming down to a later time, and a very
different day, what do *you* know of the
gradual sinking beneath consumption, or
the quick wasting of fever—the grand re-
sults of life, and dissipation—which men
have undergone in these same rooms ?
How many vain pleaders for mercy, do you
think, have turned away heart-sick from the
lawyer's office, to find a resting-place in
the Thames, or a refuge in the gaol ? They
are no ordinary houses, those. There is
not a panel in the old wainscoting but
what, if it were endowed with the powers of
speech and memory, could start from the
wall and tell its tale of horror—the romance
of life, sir, the romance of life ! Common-
place as they may seem now, I tell you

they are strange old places, and I would rather hear many a legend with a terrific-sounding name than the true history of one old set of chambers."

There was something so odd in the old man's sudden energy, and the subject which had called it forth, that Mr. Pickwick was prepared with no observation in reply; and the old man checking his impetuosity, and resuming the leer, which had disappeared during his previous excitement, said,—

" Look at them in another light ; their most common-place and least romantic. What fine places of slow torture they are ! Think of the needy man who has spent his all, beggared himself and pinched his friends to enter the profession, which will never yield him a morsel of bread. The waiting—the hope—the disappointment—the fear—the misery—the poverty—the blight on his hopes and end to his career —the suicide, perhaps, or the shabby, slip-shod drunkard. Am I not right about them?" And the old man rubbed his hands, and leered as if in delight at having found another point of view in which to place his favourite subject.

Mr. Pickwick eyed the old man with great curiosity, and the remainder of the company smiled, and looked on in silence.

" Talk of your German universities," said the little old man. " Pooh! pooh! there's romance enough at home without going half a mile for it; only people never think of it."

" I never thought of the romance of this particular subject before, certainly," said Mr. Pickwick, laughing.

" To be sure you didn't," said the little old man, " of course not. As a friend of mine used to say to me, ' What is there in chambers in particular?' ' Queer old places,' said I. ' Not at all,' said he. ' Lonely,' said I. ' Not a bit of it,' said he. He died one morning of apoplexy, as he was going to open his outer door. Fell

3

with his head in his own letter-box, and
there he lay for eighteen months. Everybody thought he'd gone out of town.

"And how was he found out at last?"
inquired Mr. Pickwick.

"The benchers determined to have his
door broken open, as he hadn't paid any
rent for two years. So they did. Forced
the lock; and a very dusty skeleton in a
blue coat, black knee-shorts, and silks, fell
forward in the arms of the porter who
opened the door. Queer, that. Rather,
perhaps?" The little old man put his
head more on one side, and rubbed his
hands with unspeakable glee.

"I know another case," said the little
old man, when his chuckles had in some
degree subsided. "It occurred in Clif-
ford's Inn. Tenant of a top set—bad
character—shut himself up in his bedroom
closet, and took a dose of arsenic. The
steward thought he had run away; opened
the door and put a bill up. Another man

came, took the chambers, furnished them,
and went to live there. Somehow or other
he couldn't sleep—always restless and uncomfortable. 'Odd,' says he. 'I'll make
the other room my bedchamber, and this
my sitting-room.' He made the change,
and slept very well at night, but suddenly
found that, somehow, he couldn't read in
the evening; he got nervous and uncomfortable, and used to be always snuffing
his candles and staring about him. 'I
can't make this out,' said he, when he
came home from the play one night, and
was drinking a glass of cold grog, with his
back to the wall, in order that he mightn't
be able to fancy there was any one behind
him—'I can't make it out,' said he; and
just then his eyes rested on the little closet
that had been always locked up, and a
shudder ran through his whole frame from
top to toe. 'I have felt this strange feeling before,' said he. 'I can't help thinking there's something wrong about that

closet.' He made a strong effort, plucked
up his courage, shivered the lock with a
blow or two of the poker, opened the door,
and there, sure enough, standing bolt upright in the corner, was the last tenant,
with a little bottle clasped firmly in his
hand, and his face—well!" As the little
old man concluded he looked round
on the attentive faces of his wondering auditory with a smile of grim
delight.

"What strange things these are you tell
us of, sir," said Mr. Pickwick, minutely
scanning the old man's countenance by the
aid of his glasses.

"Strange!" said the little old man.
"Nonsense; you think them strange
because you know nothing about it. They
are funny, but not uncommon."

"Funny!" exclaimed Mr. Pickwick,
involuntarily.

"Yes, funny, are they not?" replied the
little old man, with a diabolical leer; and

then, without pausing for an answer, he
continued,—

"I knew another man—let me see—
forty years ago now—who took an old,
damp, rotten set of chambers in one of
the most ancient Inns, that had been shut
up and empty for years and years before.
There were lots of old women's stories
about the place, and it certainly was very
far from being a cheerful one ; but he was
poor, and the rooms were cheap, and that
would have been quite a sufficient reason
for him, if they had been ten times worse
than they really were. He was obliged to
take some mouldering fixtures that were
on the place, and, among the rest, was a
great lumbering wooden press for papers,
with large glass doors, and a green curtain
inside ; a pretty useless thing for him, for
he had no papers to put in it ; and as to
his clothes, he carried them about with
him, and that wasn't very hard work either.
Well, he had moved in all his furniture—

it wasn't quite a truck-full—and had sprinkled it about the room, so as to make the four chairs look as much like a dozen as possible, and was sitting down before the fire at night, drinking the first glass of two gallons of whisky he had ordered on credit, wondering whether it would ever be paid for, and if so, in how many years' time, when his eyes encountered the glass doors of the wooden press. 'Ah,' says he, 'if I hadn't been obliged to take that ugly article at the old broker's valuation I might have got something comfortable for the money. I'll tell you what it is, old fellow,' he said, speaking aloud to the press, having nothing else to speak to, 'if it wouldn't cost more to break up your old carcase than it would ever be worth afterwards, I'd have a fire out of you in less than no time.' He had hardly spoken the words when a sound, resembling a faint groan, appeared to issue from the interior of the case. It startled him at first, but thinking, on a moment's reflection, that it must be some young fellow in the next chamber, who had been dining out, he put his feet on the fender, and raised the poker to stir the fire.   At that moment the sound was repeated, and one of the glass doors slowly opening disclosed a pale and emaciated figure in soiled and worn apparel standing erect in the press.   The figure was tall and thin, and the counten- ance expressive of care and anxiety; but there was something in the hue of the skin, and gaunt and unearthly appearance of the whole form, which no being of this world was ever seen to wear.   'Who are you?' said the new tenant, turning very pale, poising the poker in his hand, how- ever, and taking a very decent aim at the countenance of the figure.   'Who are you?'   'Don't throw that poker at me,' replied the form.   'If you hurled it with ever so sure an aim, it would pass through me without resistance, and expend its force

on the wood behind. I am a spirit.' 'And,
pray, what do you want here?' faltered
the tenant. ' In this room,' replied the
apparition, ' my worldly ruin was worked,
and I and my children beggared. In this
press the papers in a long, long suit, which
accumulated for years, were deposited. In
this room, when I had died of grief and
long-deferred hope, two wily harpies
divided the wealth for which I had contested during a wretched existence, and of
which, at last, not one farthing was left for
my unhappy descendants. I terrified them
from the spot, and since that day have
prowled by night—the only period
at which I can re-visit the earth—
about the scenes of my long-protracted
misery. This apartment is mine; leave
it to me.' ' If you insist on making your
appearance here,' said the tenant, who
had time to collect his presence of mind
during this prosy statement of the ghost's,
' I shall give up possession with the greatest

pleasure ; but I should like to ask you one
question, if you will allow me.' 'Say on,'
said the apparition, sternly. 'Well,' said
the tenant, ' I don't apply the observation
personally to you, because it is equally
applicable to most of the ghosts I ever
heard of; but it does appear to me some-
what inconsistent that when you have an
opportunity of visiting the fairest spots
of earth—for I suppose space is nothing to
you—you should always return exactly to
the very places where you have been most
miserable.' 'Egad, that's very true; I never
thought of that before,' said the ghost.
'You see, sir,' pursued the tenant, 'this
is a very uncomfortable room. From the
appearance of that press I should be disposed to say that it is not wholly free from
bugs ; and I really think you might find
much more comfortable quarters, to say
nothing of the climate of London, which
is extremely disagreeable.' 'You are very
right, sir,' said the ghost, politely; 'it never

struck me till now ; I'll try a change of air
directly.' In fact, he began to vanish as
he spoke—his legs, indeed, had quite disappeared. 'And if, sir,' said the tenant,
calling after him, 'if you *would* have the
goodness to suggest to the other ladies
and gentlemen who are now engaged in
haunting old empty houses, that they
might be much more comfortable elsewhere,
you will confer a very great benefit on
society.' 'I will,' replied the ghost; 'we
must be dull fellows, very dull fellows
indeed ; I can't imagine how we can have
been so stupid.' With these words the
spirit disappeared ; and what is rather
remarkable," added the old man, with a
shrewd look round the table, " he never
came back again."

But I must not delay longer over
where the lawyers live. The lawyers
of Dickens furnish me with three types
of the practising solicitor or attorney,

each admirable in its way. First, Mr. Perker, whose aid Mr. Wardle seeks to release Miss Rachel Wardle from that scoundrel Jingle. He is described as a little high-dried man, with a dark squeezed-up face, and small restless black eyes, that kept winking and twinkling on each side of his little inquisitive nose, as if they were playing a perpetual game of peep-bo with that feature. He was dressed all in black, with boots as shiny as his eyes, a low white neckcloth, and a clean shirt with a frill to it. A gold watch-chain and seals depended from his fob. He carried his black kid gloves *in* his hands, and not *on* them ; and as he spoke, thrust his wrists beneath his coat-tails, with the air of a man who was in the habit of propounding some regular posers.

He lived at Montague Place, Rus-

sell Square, and had offices in Gray's
Inn, and appears to have had a large
and very respectable business, into
the details of which we have not time
to travel ; but perhaps the cleverest
piece of business he ever did was
when, as Agent to the Honourable
Samuel Slumkey, of Slumkey Hall,
he brought about the return of that
honourable gentleman as Member of
Parliament. I suppose we have all
read the account of that memorable
election, which is a pretty accurate
record of what went on at Eatanswill,
and I am credibly informed at many
other places.

Mr. Pickwick and his companions,
in their quest for experience, set out
for the excitement of a contested
election, and found their way to the
agent's room.

" Ah—ah, my dear sir," said the little

man, advancing to meet him; "very
happy to see you, my dear sir, very. Pray
sit down. So you have carried your
intention into effect. You have come
down here to see an election—eh?"

Mr. Pickwick replied in the affirma-
tive.

"Spirited contest, my dear sir," said the
little man.

"I'm delighted to hear it," said Mr.
Pickwick, rubbing his hands. "I like to
see sturdy patriotism, on whatever side it
is called forth;—and so it's a spirited
contest?"

"Oh, yes," said the little man, "very
much so indeed. We have opened all the
public-houses in the place, and left our
adversary nothing but the beer-shops—
masterly stroke of policy that, my dear
sir, eh?"

The little man smiled complacently, and
took a large pinch of snuff.

"And what are the probabilities as

to the result of the contest?" inquired
Mr. Pickwick.

"Why, doubtful, my dear sir; rather
doubtful as yet," replied the little man.
" Fizkin's people have got three-and-thirty
voters in the lock-up coach-house at the
White Hart."

" In the coach-house !" said Mr. Pickwick, considerably astonished by this second
stroke of policy.

" They keep 'em locked up there till they
want 'em," resumed the little man. " The
effect of that is, you see, to prevent our
getting at them ; and even if we could, it
would be of no use, for they keep them
very drunk on purpose. Smart fellow
Fizkin's agent—very smart fellow indeed."

Mr. Pickwick stared, but said nothing.

" We are pretty confident, though," said
Mr. Perker, sinking his voice almost to a
whisper. " We had a little tea-party here

last night—five-and-forty women, my dear
sir—and gave every one of 'em a green
parasol when she went away."

"A parasol?" said Mr. Pickwick.

"Fact, my dear sir, fact. Five-and-forty
green parasols at seven and sixpence
a-piece. All women like finery—extraordinary the effect of those parasols.
Secured all their husbands, and half their
brothers—beat stockings, and flannel, and
all that sort of thing hollow. My idea, my
dear sir, entirely. Hail, rain, or sunshine,
you can't walk half-a-dozen yards up the
street without encountering half-a-dozen
green parasols."

On the day of the election the stable yard
exhibited unequivocal symptoms of the
glory and strength of the Eatanswill Blues.
There was a regular army of blue flags,
some with one handle, and some with two,
exhibiting appropriate devices, in golden
characters four feet high, and stout in pro-
portion. There was a grand band of

trumpets, bassoons, and drums, marshalled four abreast, and earning their money, if ever men did, especially the drum beaters, who were very muscular. There were bodies of constables with blue staves, twenty committee men with blue scarves, and a mob of voters with blue cockades. There were electors on horseback and electors on foot. There was an open carriage and four, for the Honourable Samuel Slumkey; and there were four carriages and pair, for his friends and supporters; and the flags were rustling, and the band was playing, and the constables were swearing, and the twenty committee men were squabbling, and the mob were shouting, and the horses were backing, and the post-boys were perspiring; and everybody, and everything, then and there assembled, was for the special use, behoof, honour, and renown, of the Honourable Samuel Slumkey, of Slumkey Hall, one of the candidates for the representation of the Borough of Eatanswill, in the Commons House of Parliament of the United Kingdom.

Loud and long were the cheers, and mighty was the rustling of one of the blue flags, with "Liberty of the Press" inscribed thereon, when the sandy head of Mr. Pott was discerned in one of the windows by the mob beneath ; and tremendous was the enthusiasm when the Honourable Samuel Slumkey himself, in top boots, and a blue neckerchief, advanced and seized the hand of the said Pott, and melodramatically testified by gestures to the crowd his ineffaceable obligations to the *Eatanswill Gazette*.

"Is everything ready?" said the Honourable Samuel Slumkey to Mr. Perker.

" Everything, my dear sir," was the little man's reply.

" Nothing has been omitted, I hope ? " said the Honourable Samuel Slumkey.

"Nothing has been left undone, my dear sir—nothing whatever. There are

4

twenty washed men at the street door
for you to shake hands with; and six
children in arms that you're to pat on the
head, and inquire the age of; be particular about the children, my dear sir,—
it has always a great effect, that sort of
thing."

"I'll take care," said the Honourable
Samuel Slumkey.

"And perhaps, my dear sir," said the
cautious little man, "perhaps if you *could*
—I don't mean to say it's indispensable—
but if you *could* manage to kiss one of 'em
it would produce a very great impression
on the crowd."

"Wouldn't it have as good an effect if
the proposer or seconder did that?" said
the Honourable Samuel Slumkey.

"Why, I am afraid it wouldn't," replied
the agent; "if it were done by yourself,
my dear sir, I think it would make you
very popular."

"Very well," said the Honourable

Samuel Slumkey, with a resigned air, "then it must be done. That's all."

"Arrange the procession," cried the twenty committee men.

Amidst the cheers of the assembled throng, the band, and the constables, and the committee men, and the voters, and the horsemen, and the carriages took their places—each of the two-horse vehicles being closely packed with as many gentlemen as could manage to stand upright in it; and that assigned to Mr. Perker containing Mr. Pickwick, Mr. Tupman, Mr. Snodgrass, and about half-a-dozen of the committee beside.

There was a moment of awful suspense as the procession waited for the Honourable Samuel Slumkey to step into his carriage. Suddenly the crowd set up a great cheering.

"He has come out," said little Mr. Perker, greatly excited; the more so as their position did not enable them to see what was going forward.

Another cheer, much louder.

" He has shaken hands with the men,"
cried the little agent.

Another cheer, far more vehement.

" He has patted the babies on the head,"
said Mr. Perker, trembling with anxiety.

A roar of applause that rent the air.

" He has kissed one of 'em ! " exclaimed
the delighted little man.

A second roar.

" He has kissed another," gasped the
excited manager.

A third roar.

" He's kissing 'em all ! " screamed the
enthusiastic little gentleman.   And hailed
by the deafening shouts of the multitude
the procession moved on.

Ladies and gentlemen, according to
our modern ideas this account does
not do much to raise Mr. Perker in
our estimation ; but the best testi-
monial to his memory is to be found

in Mr. Pickwick's observation when, being at last free from all his legal difficulties, he proposed to settle up with his lawyer.

"Well, now," said Mr. Pickwick, "let me have a settlement with you."

"Of the same kind as the last?" inquired Perker, with another laugh, for Mr. Pickwick had just been dismissing Messrs. Dodson and Fogg with some strong language indeed.

"Not exactly," said Mr. Pickwick, drawing out his pocket-book, and shaking the little man heartily by the hand; "I only mean a pecuniary settlement. You have done me many acts of kindness that I can never repay, and have no wish to repay, for I prefer continuing the obligation."

With this preface the two friends dived into some very complicated accounts and vouchers, which, having been duly displayed and gone through by Perker, were at once discharged by Mr. Pickwick with many professions of esteem and friendship.

Never was bill of costs so pleasantly discharged, though I know many lawyers who have won the friendship and esteem of their clients.

The next type is that of Messrs. Dodson and Fogg, of Freeman's Court, Cornhill. The character of the genial partner is best described by one of his clerks in a conversation overheard by Mr. Pickwick and Sam Weller while waiting for an interview with this celebrated firm.

"There was such a game with Fogg here this morning," said the man in the brown coat, "while Jack was upstairs sorting the papers, and you two were gone to the stamp-office. Fogg was down here

opening the letters when that chap as we
issued the writ against at Camberwell, you
know, came in—what's his name again ? "

" Ramsey," said the clerk who had
spoken to Mr. Pickwick.

" Ah, Ramsey—a precious seedy-look-
ing customer. ' Well, sir,' says old Fogg,
looking at him very fierce—you know his
way—' well, sir, have you come to settle ? '
' Yes, I have, sir,' said Ramsey, putting his
hand in his pocket and bringing out the
money ; " the debt's two pound ten, and
the costs three pound five, and here it is,
sir,' and he sighed like bricks as he lugged
out the money, done up in a bit of blotting-
paper. Old Fogg looked first at the money,
and then at him, and then he coughed
in his rum way, so that I knew something
was coming. ' You don't know there's a
declaration filed, which increases the costs
materially, I suppose ? ' said Fogg. ' You
don't say that, sir,' said Ramsey, starting
back ; ' the time was only out last night,

sir.' 'I do say it, though,' said Fogg;
'my clerk's just gone to file it. Hasn't
Mr. Jackson gone to file that declaration
in Bullman and Ramsey, Mr. Wicks?'
Of course I said yes, and then Fogg
coughed again, and looked at Ramsey.
'My God!' said Ramsey; 'and here have
I nearly driven myself mad, scraping this
money together, and all to no purpose.'
'None at all,' said Fogg, coolly; 'so you
had better go back and scrape some more
together, and bring it here in time.' 'I
can't get it, by God!' said Ramsey, strik-
ing the desk with his fist. 'Don't bully
me, sir,' said Fogg, getting into a passion
on purpose. 'I am not bullying you,
sir,' said Ramsey. 'You are,' said Fogg;
'get out, sir; get out of this office, sir,
and come back, sir, when you know how
to behave yourself.' Well, Ramsey tried
to speak, but Fogg wouldn't let him, so he
put the money in his pocket and sneaked
out. The door was scarcely shut when

old Fogg turned round to me, with a sweet smile on his face, and drew the declaration out of his coat pocket. 'Here, Wicks,' said Fogg, 'take a cab and go down to the Temple as quick as you can and file that. The costs are quite safe, for he's a steady man with a large family, at a salary of five-and-twenty shillings a week; and if he gives us a warrant of attorney, as he must in the end, I know his employers will see it paid, so we may as well get all we can out of him, Mr. Wicks; it's a Christian act to do it, Mr. Wicks, for with his large family and small income he'll be all the better for a good lesson against getting into debt—won't he, Mr. Wicks, won't he?' and he smiled so good-naturedly as he went away that it was delightful to see him. 'He is a capital man of business,' said Wicks, in a tone of the deepest admiration; 'capital, isn't he?'"

Mr. Fogg, we are told, was an elderly, pimply-faced, vegetable diet

sort of man, in a black coat, and dark-
mixtured trousers ; and Mr. Dodson
was a plump, portly, stern-looking
man, with a loud voice. And it was
from these worthies that Mr. Pickwick had received a letter dated the
28th of August, 1827.

Freeman's Court, Cornhill.
Bardell against Pickwick.

Sir,—Having been instructed by Mrs.
Martha Bardell to commence an action
against you for a breach of promise of
marriage, for which the plaintiff lays her
damages at fifteen hundred pounds, we beg
to inform you that a writ has been issued
against you in this suit in the Court of
Common Pleas, and request to know, by
return of post, the name of your attorney
in London, who will accept service thereof.

We are, Sir,
Your obedient servants,
Dodson and Fogg.

Mr. Samuel Pickwick.

I am bound to say that Mr. Pickwick did not conduct himself with his
usual dignity on the occasion of his
interview on the subject of this letter.
The two sharp practitioners had certainly commenced an action against
him on grounds which, though
definite, were wholly inadequate.
But in this alone there was nothing
to justify the very violent language
of Mr. Pickwick.

"Very well, gentlemen, very well," said
Mr. Pickwick, rising in person and wrath
at the same time; "you shall hear from
my solicitor, gentlemen."

"We shall be very happy to do so,"
said Fogg, rubbing his hands.

"Very," said Dodson, opening the
door.

"And before I go, gentlemen," said
the excited Mr. Pickwick, turning round
on the landing, "permit me to say,

that of all the disgraceful and rascally proceedings——"

"Stay, sir, stay," interposed Dodson, with great politeness. "Mr. Jackson! Mr. Wicks!"

"Sir," said the two clerks, appearing at the bottom of the stairs.

"I merely want you to hear what this gentleman says," replied Dodson. "Pray go on, sir—disgraceful and rascally proceedings, I think you said?"

"I did," said Mr. Pickwick, thoroughly roused. "I said, sir, that of all the disgraceful and rascally proceedings that ever were attempted this is the most so. I repeat it, sir."

"You hear that, Mr. Wicks?" said Dodson.

"You won't forget these expressions, Mr. Jackson?" said Fogg.

"Perhaps you would like to call us swindlers, sir," said Dodson. "Pray do, sir, if you feel disposed; now pray do, sir."

"I do," said Mr. Pickwick. "You *are* swindlers."

"Very good," said Dodson. "You can hear down there, I hope, Mr. Wicks?"

"Oh, yes, sir," said Wicks.

"You had better come up a step or two higher if you can't," added Mr. Fogg. "Go on, sir; do go on. You had better call us thieves, sir; or perhaps you would like to assault one of us. Pray do it, sir, if you would; we will not make the slightest resistance. Pray do it, sir."

As Fogg put himself very temptingly within the reach of Mr. Pickwick's clenched fist there is little doubt that gentleman would have complied with his earnest entreaty but for the interposition of Sam, who, hearing the dispute, emerged from the office, mounted the stairs, and seized his master by the arm.

"You just come avay," said Mr. Weller. "Battledore and shuttlecock's a wery good game, when you ain't the

shuttlecock and two lawyers the battle-
dores, in which case it gets too excitin'
to be pleasant. Come avay, sir. If you
want to ease your mind by blowing up
somebody come out into the court and
blow up me; but it's rayther too expensive
work to be carried on here."

With that good advice Mr. Weller
took Mr. Pickwick away from the
lawyers' office. But before we say
anything about the trial itself let
me introduce to you another solicitor
not so well known as either Perker
or Dodson and Fogg, but to my mind
the most interesting as he certainly
is the most humorous.

Mr. Pell had the honour of being
the legal adviser of Mr. Weller,
Senior. The latter gentleman always
stoutly maintained that if Mr. Pickwick had had the services of Mr.
Pell, and had established an *alibi*,

the great case of Bardell against
Pickwick would have been decided
otherwise. Mr. Pell practised in
the Insolvency Court. He " was a fat,
flabby, pale man, in a surtout which
looked green one moment, and brown
the next, with a velvet collar of the
same chameleon tints. His forehead
was narrow, his face wide, his head
large, and his nose all on one side,
as if Nature, indignant with the pro-
pensities she observed in him at his
birth, had given it an angry tweak
which it had never recovered. Being
short-necked and asthmatic, however,
he respired principally through this
feature ; so, perhaps, what it wanted
in ornament, it made up in useful-
ness."

Mr. Pell had successfully piloted
Mr. Weller through the Insolvency
Court, and his services were sought

to carry out the process by which
Sam Weller became a voluntary
prisoner in the Fleet at the suit of
his obdurate parent.

"The late Lord Chancellor, gentlemen,
was very fond of me," said Mr. Pell.

"And wery creditable in him, too," interposed Mr. Weller.

'Hear, hear," assented Mr. Pell's client.
"Why shouldn't he be?"

"Ah, why, indeed!" said a very red-
faced man, who had said nothing yet, and
who looked extremely unlikely to say anything more. "Why shouldn't he?"

A murmur of assent ran through the
company.

"I remember, gentlemen," said Mr.
Pell, "dining with him on one occasion.
There was only us two, but everything as
splendid as if twenty people had been
expected—the great seal on a dumb-waiter
at his right, and a man in a bag-wig and

suit of armour guarding the mace with a drawn sword and silk stockings—which is perpetually done, gentlemen, night and day; when he said, 'Pell,' he said, 'no false delicacy, Pell. You're a man of talent; you can get anybody through the Insolvent Court, Pell; and your country should be proud of you.' Those were his very words. 'My lord,' I said, ' you flatter me.' 'Pell,' he said, 'if I do I'm damned.'"

"Did he say that?" inquired Mr. Weller.

"He did," replied Pell.

"Vell, then," said Mr. Weller, "I say Parliament ought to ha' took it up; and if he'd been a poor man they *would* ha' done it."

"But, my dear friend," argued Mr. Pell, "it was in confidence."

"In what?" said Mr. Weller.

"In confidence."

"Oh! wery good," replied Mr. Weller,

after a little reflection. "If he damned
hisself in confidence, o' course that was
another thing."

"Of course it was," said Mr. Pell. "The
distinction's obvious, you will perceive."

"Alters the case entirely," said Mr.
Weller. "Go on, sir."

"No, I will not go on, sir," said Mr.
Pell, in a low and serious tone. "You
have reminded me, sir, that this conversation was private—private and confidential,
gentlemen. Gentlemen, I am a professional man. It may be that I am a good
deal looked up to in my profession—it
may be that I am not. Most people know.
I say nothing. Observations have already
been made in this room injurious to the
reputation of my noble friend. You will
excuse me, gentlemen; I was imprudent.
I feel that I have no right to mention this
matter without his concurrence. Thank
you, sir; thank you."

Thus delivering himself, Mr. Pell thrust

his hands into his pockets, and, frowning grimly around, rattled three-halfpence with terrible determination.

We hear also of Mrs. Pell.

Mrs. Pell was a tall figure, a splendid woman, with a noble shape, and a nose, gentlemen, formed to command, gentlemen, and be majestic. She was very much attached to me—very much—highly connected, too. Her mother's brother, gentlemen, failed for eight hundred pounds, as a law stationer.

So we have, ladies and gentlemen, these three types of this honourable profession. To my mind they have never been quite placed in their proper order. Perker has been universally admired and looked up to ; Dodson and Fogg have been universally denounced ; Mr. Pell has been suffered to remain unnoticed. Well, let us judge fairly the merits of these three gentlemen.

If Mr. Perker had lived to-day instead of in the year 1827, he would undoubtedly have been tried for the part he took in the Eatanswill election. What is the charge, after all, against Messrs. Dodson and Fogg, except that question with regard to poor Ramsey?—which, after all, is only a story told by the clerk Wicks, upon whom I do not think we can place very much reliance. What else did Dodson and Fogg do that should make them the object of obloquy and universal execration? They brought an action for breach of promise of marriage—some people think such actions should never be brought at all—they brought the action for breach of promise of marriage ; they made a little arrangement with regard

to costs, unprofessional if you like,
but still nothing to bring down upon
them the denouncement to which they
have been made subject. So far as
Mr. Pickwick was concerned, he had
absolutely nothing to complain of in
their conduct ; and I venture to say
it was most reprehensible in him
under the circumstances to use the
language which he did upon the occasion which I have quoted. But
against Mr. Pell there is absolutely
nothing to be said. He perhaps
romanced a little with regard to his
friendship with the Lord Chancellor ;
but which of us would not like to
be on friendly terms with the Lord
Chancellor ? On that trifling exag-
geration there is nothing practically
to be urged against him ; and while I
claim for Mr. Pell the position of
premier in this matter, I am sorry I

have to accord to Mr. Perker the third place.

Well, now, although I would love to linger over Mr. Pell, I must pass on to say something of the counsel mentioned in this admirable work. But before I consider the more eminent and the more conspicuous of these, there is one member of the Bar who is seldom alluded to, but of whom I wish to say something to-night. I refer to Mr. Prosee. Mr. Prosee very few of you have ever heard of. He dined with Mr. Perker at Montague Place, Russell Square, on one occasion. It must have been rather a dull dinner party, for there were present two good country agents, Mr. Snicks, the Life Office Secretary, Mr. Prosee, the eminent counsel, three solicitors, one Commissioner of Bankrupts, a special pleader from the Temple, a

small-eyed, peremptory young gentleman, his pupil, who had written a
lively book about the law of demises,
with a vast quantity of marginal notes
and references ; and several other
eminent and distinguished person-
ages, including the Mr. Prosee just
mentioned.

Ladies and gentlemen, I do not
know how it is, but I have always
associated Mr. Prosee with the Equity
Bar. It may be that his name sug-
gests it.

Well, I come now to the counsel
who is better known to you, namely
Serjeant Snubbin.

" We've done everything that's necessary," said Mr. Perker. " I have retained
Serjeant Snubbin."

" Is he a good man ? " inquired Mr.
Pickwick.

" Good man ! " replied Perker. " Bless

your heart and soul, my dear sir, Serjeant
Snubbin is at the very top of his profession.
Gets treble the business of any man in
court—engaged in every case.   You
needn't mention it abroad, but we say—
we of the profession—that Serjeant Snubbin
leads the court by the nose."

"I should like to see him," said Mr.
Pickwick.

"See Serjeant Snubbin, my dear sir!"
rejoined Perker, in utter amazement.
"Pooh, pooh! my dear sir, impossible!
See Serjeant Snubbin! Bless you, my dear
sir, such a thing was never heard of without a consultation fee being previously
paid, and a consultation fixed. It couldn't
be done, my dear sir—it couldn't be
done!"

Thus was Mr. Pickwick brought
face to face with the difficulty of
seeing his own counsel. He could
not understand why, having retained

the services of a professional man and paid for them, there should exist any impediment to prevent access to him. I won't discuss to-night the advisability or non-advisability of dividing the profession of the law into two parts, but I do say that any system which prevents litigants having the fullest personal communication with those they have paid to represent them is an anomaly and an absurdity.

But Mr. Pickwick was a person of determination, and he did see Serjeant Snubbin, and he delivered to that learned gentleman a short address that was well worthy of his attention, as it is of every member of the Bar, including your very humble servant.

"Gentlemen of your profession, sir," continued Mr. Pickwick, "see the worst

side of human nature.   All its disputes, all
its ill-will and bad blood, rise up before you.
You know from your experience of juries
(I mean no disparagement to you, or them)
how much depends upon *effect*; and you
are apt to attribute to others a desire to use,
for purposes of deception and self-interest,
the very instruments which you, in pure
honesty and honour of purpose, and with a
laudable desire to do your utmost for your
client, know the temper and worth of so
well, from constantly employing them your-
selves.   I really believe that to this circum-
stance may be attributed the vulgar but
very general notion of your being, as a
body, suspicious, distrustful, and over-
cautious.   Conscious as I am, sir, of the
disadvantage of making such a declaration
to you, under such circumstances, I have
come here, because I wish you distinctly
to understand, as my friend Mr. Perker
has said, that I am innocent of the false-
hood laid to my charge ; and although I

am very well aware of the inestimable value of your assistance, sir, I must beg to add that, unless you sincerely believe this, I would rather be deprived of the aid of your talents than have the advantage of them."

The only effect this had upon Serjeant Snubbin was to cause him to ask rather snappishly,—

" Who is with me in this case ? "

" Mr. Phunky, Serjeant Snubbin," replied the attorney.

" Phunky, Phunky," said the Serjeant, " I never heard the name before. He must be a very young man."

" Yes, he is a very young man," replied the attorney. " He was only called the other day. Let me see—he has not been at the Bar eight years yet."

" Ah, I thought not," said the Serjeant, in that sort of pitying tone in which ordinary folks would speak of a very helpless little child. " Mr. Mallard, send round to Mr.—Mr.——"

" Phunky's — Holborn Court, Gray's
Inn," interposed Perker. (Holborn Court,
by-the-bye, is South Square now.)

" Mr. Phunky, and say I should be glad
if he'd step here a moment."

Mr. Mallard departed to execute his
commission, and Serjeant Snubbin relapsed
into abstraction until Mr. Phunky himself
was introduced.

Although an infant barrister he was a
full-grown man. He had a very nervous
manner, and a painful hesitation in his
speech ; it did not appear to be a natural
defect, but seemed rather the result of
timidity, arising from the consciousness of
being " kept down " by want of means, or
interest, or connection, or impudence, as
the case might be. He was overawed by
the Serjeant, and profoundly courteous to
the attorney.

" I have not had the pleasure of seeing
you before, Mr. Phunky," said Serjeant
Snubbin, with haughty condescension.

Mr. Phunky bowed. He *had* had the pleasure of seeing the Serjeant, and of envying him too, with all a poor man's envy, for eight years and a quarter.

"You are with me in this case, I understand?" said the Serjeant.

If Mr. Phunky had been a rich man he would have instantly sent for his clerk to remind him; if he had been a wise one he would have applied his forefinger to his forehead, and endeavoured to recollect whether, in the multiplicity of his engagements, he had undertaken this one or not; but as he was neither rich nor wise (in this sense, at all events) he turned red and bowed.

"Have you read the papers, Mr. Phunky?" inquired the Serjeant.

Here again Mr. Phunky should have professed to have forgotten all about the merits of the case; but as he had read such papers as had been laid before him in the course of the action, and had thought

of nothing else, waking or sleeping, throughout the two months during which he had
been retained as Mr. Serjeant Snubbin's
junior, he turned a deeper red and bowed
again.

"This is Mr. Pickwick," said the Serjeant, waving his pen in the direction in
which that gentleman was standing.

Mr. Phunky bowed to Mr. Pickwick
with a reverence which a first client must
ever awaken, and again inclined his head
towards his leader.

"Perhaps you will take Mr. Pickwick
away," said the Serjeant, " and—and—and
—hear anything Mr. Pickwick may wish
to communicate. We shall have a consultation, of course." With this hint that
he had been interrupted quite long enough,
Mr. Serjeant Snubbin, who had been
gradually growing more and more ab-
stracted, applied his glass to his eye for
an instant, bowed slightly round, and was
once more deeply immersed in the case

before him, which arose out of an interminable law-suit originating in the act of an individual, deceased a century or so ago, who had stopped up a pathway leading from some place which nobody ever came from to some other place which nobody ever went to.

Mr. Phunky would not hear of passing through any door until Mr. Pickwick and his solicitor had passed through before him, so it was some time before they got into the Square ; and when they did reach it they walked up and down, and held a long conference, the result of which was that it was a very difficult matter to say how the verdict would go ; that nobody could presume to calculate on the issue of an action ; that it was very lucky they had prevented the other party from getting Serjeant Snubbin ; and other topics of doubt and consolation common in such a position of affairs.

Mr. Pickwick's lawsuit was to be

tried in the Court of Common Pleas, a division in which Serjeants-at-Law had the exclusive right to practise. At this time, 1827, and indeed up till 1873, every common law judge was turned into a Serjeant, if he were not one ere he was promoted to the Bench. It was a solemn kind of ceremony. The subject of the operation was led out of the precincts of the Inns of Court ; the church bell tolled as for one dead.

He was then admitted member of Serjeants' Inn ; and the judge would address the serjeants who practised before him as Brother So-and-So. Justice Lindley was the last judge who took the degree, a degree the only outward visible sign of which is the black patch or coif which is attached to the top of the wig. I do not know what kind of counsel

Serjeant Snubbin, retained by Mr.
Perker for the defendant, was ; but
Dodson and Fogg had retained
Serjeant Buzfuz for the plaintiff, and
we all know that Serjeant Snubbin
was no match for Serjeant Buzfuz.
It has been objected by a writer in
Fraser's Magazine, to the account
of this trial, that it is full of in-
consistencies. Serjeant Buzfuz' case,
he says, was absurd, and that he
would not have been able to brow-
beat any witness, and that no jury
could have given a verdict on such
evidence. This criticism resembles
many other criticisms of Pickwick.
Had the description in Pickwick been
intended as a serious picture of the
proceedings in a court of justice, it
would have been open to much
serious dissection and examination.

But the writer just quoted did not,

6

it seems, possess a sufficient sense of humour to enable him to see that this chapter of " Pickwick " was intended for broad fun amounting to burlesque, and nothing more ; and to examine Mr. Buzfuz' proceedings by the light of the law is to strip them of their meaning.

I mentioned just now that this trial took place in 1827. At that time, as I daresay some of you are aware, the parties to the action could not be called upon to give evidence ; and Lord Denman did not, I think, till 1843 remove the Arcadian fetters which bound the litigants in this fashion. But, ladies and gentlemen, what a fortunate thing it was for Mr. Pickwick that he could not be called upon that occasion. If Mr. Pickwick had been called he would have been cross-examined. Let us imagine for

a moment what that cross-examination
would have been. Suppose merely
for the sake of example that that
operation had been performed by
my honourable and learned friend
the Attorney-General. Cannot you
imagine how in the first place he
would forcibly but firmly have in-
terrogated Mr. Pickwick with regard
to his conduct after the cricket match
at Muggleton ; how he would have
asked him whether he was prepared
to admit, or whether he was prepared
to deny, that he was drunk upon that
occasion ? Could you not imagine how
my honourable and learned friend,
passing on from that topic, would
have alluded to what I think he would
have termed the disgraceful incident
when, on the 1st of September, Mr.
Pickwick was found in a wheelbarrow
on the ground of Captain Boldwig,

and was removed to the public pound,
from which he was only extricated by
the violence of his friends and servant?
Passing on from that topic, would not
my honourable and learned friend
have reminded him of how he had
been bound over at Ipswich before
Mr. Nupkins, together with his friend
Mr. Tupman, and called upon to
find bail for good behaviour for six
months? Then in conclusion how my
friend would have turned to that incident in the double-bedded room at
Ipswich, at the Great White Horse,
and how my learned friend, with that
skill which he possesses, would, bit by
bit, by slow degrees, have extricated
from that miserable man the con-
fession that he had been found in that
double-bedded room, a spinster lady
being there at the same time. Ladies
and gentlemen, what would have been

left of Mr. Pickwick after that process had been gone through? His only relief would have been to write to the *Times* newspaper, and to complain of cross-examination.

Indeed, no notice of this case, as indeed no reference to the lawyers of " Pickwick," would be regarded as in any sense complete that did not include the remarkable forensic efforts of Serjeant Buzfuz. Oft read, oft recited, oft quoted, it stands to-day, perhaps, the best-known speech ever delivered at the Bar.

We are told that the speech of Serjeant Snubbin was long and emphatic, but at any rate it was ineffective, and that learned gentleman committed a grave error in entrusting the cross-examination of Mr. Winkle to Mr. Phunky. Now it does sometimes happen, in the course of a case, that

owing to the absence of the leading
counsel, which sometimes occurs, the
cross-examination of a witness, per-
chance an important one, is left to
some junior ; but this excuse did not
exist in this case. Serjeant Snubbin
was there in Court, because we hear
that he winked at Mr. Phunky to
intimate to him that he had better sit
down ; and this, as we know, from
what I have told you just now, was
the first brief that Mr. Phunky had
ever had. No, Serjeant Snubbin was
over-matched throughout by Serjeant
Buzfuz, and Mr. Phunky was no
match even for the scheming junior
on the other side, and Perker was no
match for Dodson and Fogg. The
law, as we are told in one of George
Eliot's books, is a kind of cock-fight,
in which it is the business of injured
honesty to get a game bird with the

best pluck and the strongest spurs ;
and I venture to think that the com-
bined pluck of Buzfuz and Skimpin
by far outweighed any of that com-
modity possessed by Snubbin and
Phunky. No wonder Mr. Pickwick
lost his case ; but his case never
recovered the effect of the speech
which I now propose to read to
you.

Serjeant Buzfuz began by saying that
never, in the whole course of his professional experience—never, from the very
first moment of his applying himself to
the study and practice of the law—had he
approached a case with feelings of such
deep emotion, or with such a heavy sense
of the responsibility imposed upon him—a
responsibility, he would say, which he could
never have supported, were he not buoyed
up and sustained by a conviction so strong,
that it amounted to positive certainty that

the cause of truth and justice, or, in other
words, the cause of his much injured and
most oppressed client, must prevail with
the high-minded and intelligent dozen of
men whom he now saw in that box before
him.

Counsel usually begin in this way, because it puts the jury on the very best
terms with themselves, and makes them
think what sharp fellows they must be.   A
visible effect was produced immediately;
several jurymen beginning to take volumi-
nous notes with the utmost eagerness.

"You have heard from my learned friend,
gentlemen," continued Serjeant Buzfuz—
well knowing that, from the learned friend
alluded to, the gentlemen of the jury had
heard just nothing at all—"you have heard
from my learned friend, gentlemen, that
this is an action for breach of promise of
marriage, in which the damages are laid at
£1,500.   But you have not heard from
my learned friend, inasmuch as it did not

come within my learned friend's province
to tell you, what are the facts and circumstances of the case. Those facts and
circumstances, gentlemen, you shall hear
detailed by me, and proved by the unim-
peachable female whom I will place in that
box before you."

Here Mr. Serjeant Buzfuz, with a tremendous emphasis on the word " box,"
smote his table with a mighty sound, and
glanced at Dodson and Fogg, who nodded
admiration to the Serjeant, and indignant
defiance of the defendant.

" The plaintiff, gentlemen," continued
Serjeant Buzfuz, in a soft and melancholy
voice, " the plaintiff is a widow ; yes,
gentlemen, a widow. The late Mr. Bardell, after enjoying, for many years, the
esteem and confidence of his sovereign, as
one of the guardians of his royal revenues,
glided almost imperceptibly from the world,
to seek elsewhere for that repose and peace
which a custom house can never afford."

At this pathetic description of the decease of Mr. Bardell, who had been knocked on the head with a quart pot in a public-house cellar, the learned Serjeant's voice faltered, and he proceeded with emotion,—

"Some time before his death he had stamped his likeness upon a little boy. With this little boy, the only pledge of her departed exciseman, Mrs. Bardell shrunk from the world, and courted the retirement and tranquillity of Goswell Street; and here she placed in her front parlour-window a written placard, bearing this inscription —'Apartments furnished for a single gentleman. Inquire within.'" Here Serjeant Buzfuz paused, while several gentlemen of the jury took a note of the document.

"There is no date to that, is there?" inquired a juror.

"There is no date, gentlemen," replied Serjeant Buzfuz; "but I am instructed to say that it was put in the plaintiff's parlour-window just this time three years. *I*

entreat the attention of the jury to the
wording of this document. 'Apartments
furnished for a single gentleman!' Mrs.
Bardell's opinions of the opposite sex,
gentlemen, were derived from a long contemplation of the inestimable qualities of
her lost husband. She had no fear, she
had no distrust, she had no suspicion, all
was confidence and reliance. 'Mr. Bardell,' said the widow, 'Mr. Bardell was a
man of honour, Mr. Bardell was a man of
his word, Mr. Bardell was no deceiver,
Mr. Bardell was once a single gentleman
himself; *to* single gentlemen I look for
protection, for assistance, for comfort, and
for consolation; *in* single gentlemen I shall
perpetually see something to remind me of
what Mr. Bardell was when he first won
my young and untried affections : to a
single gentleman, then, shall my lodgings
be let.' Actuated by this beautiful and
touching impulse (among the best im-
pulses of our imperfect nature, gentlemen)

the lonely and desolate widow dried her tears, furnished her first floor, caught the innocent boy to her maternal bosom, and put the bill up in her parlour-window. Did it remain there long? No. The serpent was on the watch, the train was laid, the mine was preparing, the sapper and miner was at work. Before the bill had been in the parlour-window three days— three days, gentlemen—a Being, erect upon two legs, and bearing all the outward semblance of a man, and not of a monster, knocked at the door of Mrs. Bardell's house. He inquired within—he took the lodgings; and on the very next day he entered into possession of them. The man was Pickwick—Pickwick, the defendant."

Serjeant Buzfuz, who had proceeded with such volubility that his face was perfectly crimson, here paused for breath. The silence awoke Mr. Justice Stareleigh, who immediately wrote down something with a pen without any ink in it, and looked unusually profound, to impress the jury with the belief that he always thought most deeply with his eyes shut. Serjeant Buzfuz proceeded.

" Of this man Pickwick I will say little the subject presents but few attractions ; and I, gentlemen, am not the man, nor are you, gentlemen, the men, to delight in the contemplation of revolting heartlessness and of systematic villainy."

Here Mr. Pickwick, who had been writhing in silence for some time, gave a violent start, as if some vague idea of assaulting Serjeant Buzfuz, in the august presence of justice and law, suggested itself to his mind. An admonitory gesture from Perker restrained him, and he listened to the learned gentleman's continuation with a look of indignation, which contrasted forcibly with the admiring faces of Mrs. Cluppins and Mrs. Sanders.

" I say systematic villainy, gentlemen,"

said Serjeant Buzfuz, looking through Mr.
Pickwick, and talking *at* him ; " and when
I say systematic villainy, let me tell the
defendant Pickwick, if he be in Court—as
I am informed he is—that it would have
been more decent in him, more becoming,
in better judgment, and in better taste, if
he had stopped away. Let me tell him,
gentlemen, that any gestures of dissent or
disapprobation in which he may indulge in
this Court will not go down with you ; that
you will know how to value and how to
appreciate them ; and let me tell him
further, as my lord will tell you, gentlemen,
that a counsel, in the discharge of his duty
to his client, is neither to be intimidated,
nor bullied, nor put down ; and that any
attempt to do either the one or the other,
or the first, or the last, will recoil on the
head of the attempter, be he plaintiff or be
he defendant, be his name Pickwick, or
Noakes, or Stoakes, or Stiles, or Brown, or
Thompson."

This little divergence from the subject in hand had, of course, the intended effect of turning all eyes to Mr. Pickwick. Serjeant Buzfuz, having partially recovered from the state of moral elevation into which he had lashed himself, resumed,—

"I shall show you, gentlemen, that for two years Pickwick continued to reside constantly, and without interruption or intermission, at Mrs. Bardell's house. I shall show you that Mrs. Bardell, during the whole of that time, waited on him, attended to his comforts, cooked his meals, looked out his linen for the washerwoman when it went abroad, darned, aired, and prepared it for wear, and, in short, enjoyed his fullest trust and confidence. I shall show you that, on many occasions, he gave halfpence, and on some occasions even sixpences, to her little boy; and I shall prove to you, by a witness whose testimony it will be impossible for my

learned friend to weaken or controvert,
that on one occasion he patted the boy on
the head, and, after inquiring whether he
had won any *alley tors* or *commoneys* lately
(both of which I understand to be a particular species of marbles much prized by
the youth of this town), made use of this
remarkable expression : ' How should you
like to have another father ? '   I shall
prove to you, gentlemen, that about a year
ago Pickwick suddenly began to absent
himself from home during long intervals,
as with the intention of gradually breaking
off from my client; but I shall show you
also that his resolution was not at that
time sufficiently strong, or that his better
feelings conquered, if better feelings he
has, or that the charms and accomplish-
ments of my client prevailed against his
unmanly intentions ; by proving to you
that on one occasion, when he returned
from the country, he distinctly and in
terms offered her marriage ; previously,

however, taking special care that there should be no witnesses to their solemn contract ; and I am in a situation to prove to you, on the testimony of three of his own friends—most unwilling witnesses, gentlemen—most unwilling witnesses—that on that morning he was discovered by them holding the plaintiff in his arms, and soothing her agitation by his caresses and endearment."

A visible impression was produced upon the auditors by this part of the learned Serjeant's address. Drawing forth two very small scraps of paper, he proceeded,—

" And now, gentlemen, but one word more. Two letters have passed between these parties, letters which are admitted to be in the handwriting of the defendant, and which speak volumes indeed. These letters, too, bespeak the character of the man. They are not open, fervent, eloquent epistles, breathing nothing but the language

7

of affectionate attachment. They are
covert, sly, underhanded communications;
but, fortunately, far more conclusive than
if couched in the most glowing language
and the most poetic imagery—letters that
must be viewed with a cautious and
suspicious eye—letters that were evidently
intended at the time, by Pickwick, to
mislead and delude any third parties into
whose hands they might fall. Let me
read the first:—'Garraway's, twelve o'clock.
Dear Mrs. B.—Chops and Tomato sauce;
Yours, PICKWICK.' Gentlemen, what does
this mean? Chops and Tomato sauce.
Yours, PICKWICK! Chops! Gracious
heavens! and Tomato sauce! Gentlemen, is the happiness of a sensitive and
confiding female to be trifled away by such
shallow artifices as these? The next has
no date whatever, which is in itself
suspicious. 'Dear Mrs. B., I shall not be
at home till to-morrow. Slow coach.'
And then follows this very remarkable

expression : 'Don't trouble yourself about
the warming-pan.' The warming-pan !
Why, gentlemen, who *does* trouble himself
about a warming-pan ? When was the
peace of mind of man or woman broken
or disturbed by a warming-pan, which is
in itself a harmless, a useful, and I will
add, gentlemen, a comfortable article of
domestic furniture ? Why is Mrs. Bardell
so earnestly entreated not to agitate herself
about this warming-pan, unless (as is no
doubt the case) it is a mere cover for
hidden fire—a mere substitute for some
endearing word or promise, agreeably to a
preconcerted system of correspondence,
artfully contrived by Pickwick with a view
to his contemplated desertion, and which I
am not in a condition to explain ! And
what does this allusion to the slow coach
mean ? For aught I know, it may be a
reference to Pickwick himself, who has
most unquestionably been a criminally
slow coach during the whole of this

transaction, but whose speed will now be very unexpectedly accelerated, and whose wheels, gentlemen, as he will find to his cost, will very soon be greased by you !"

Mr. Serjeant Buzfuz paused in this place to see whether the jury smiled at his joke ; but as nobody took it but the greengrocer, whose sensitiveness on the subject was very probably occasioned by his having subjected a chaise cart to the process in question on that identical morning, the learned Serjeant considered it advisable to undergo a slight relapse into the dismals before he concluded.

"But enough of this, gentlemen," said Mr. Serjeant Buzfuz, "it is difficult to smile with an aching heart ; it is ill jesting when our deepest sympathies are awakened. My client's hopes and prospects are ruined, and it is no figure of speech to say that her occupation is gone indeed. The bill is

down—but there is no tenant. Eligible
single gentlemen pass and repass—but
there is no invitation for them to inquire
within or without. All is gloom and
silence in the house ; even the voice of the
child is hushed—his infant sports are dis-
regarded when his mother weeps ; his
'alley tors' and his 'commoneys' are
alike neglected ; he forgets the long
familiar cry of 'knuckle down,' and at
tip-cheese, or odd or even, his hand is out.
But Pickwick, gentlemen, Pickwick, the
ruthless destroyer of this domestic oasis in
the desert of Goswell Street—Pickwick,
who has choked up the well and thrown
ashes on the sward—Pickwick, who comes
before you to-day with his heartless tomato
sauce and warming-pans—Pickwick still
rears his head with unblushing effrontery,
and gazes without a sigh on the ruin he
has made. Damages, gentlemen—heavy
damages—is the only punishment with
which you can visit him ; the only recom-

pense you can award to my client. And
for those damages she now appeals to an
enlightened, a high-minded, a right-feel-
ing, a conscientious, a dispassionate, a
sympathising, a contemplative jury of her
civilised countrymen."

With this beautiful peroration, Mr. Serjeant Buzfuz sat down, and Mr. Justice
Stareleigh woke up.

Of the judge of this famous case
we hear but little. He went to sleep,
and he woke up again, and he tried
to look as though he hadn't been
asleep ; in fact, he behaved very
much as judges do.

Mr. Justice Stareleigh summed up in
the old-established and most approved form.
He read as much of his notes to the jury
as he could decipher on so short a notice,
and made running comments on the evidence as he went along. If Mrs. Bardell

were right, it was perfectly clear that Mr.
Pickwick was wrong; and if they thought
the evidence of Mrs. Cluppins worthy of
credence they would believe it, and, if
they didn't, why they wouldn't. If they
were satisfied that a breach of promise of
marriage had been committed, they would
find for the plaintiff, with such damages as
they thought proper; and if, on the other
hand, it appeared to them that no promise
of marriage had ever been given, they
would find for the defendant, with no
damages at all.

So, ladies and gentlemen, in conclusion, let me point out to you how
all these types and instances of
lawyers and lawyer life have received fair and impartial considera-
tion from Charles Dickens, for which
I, at any rate, am grateful. The
public, however, to my mind, owe
a deeper debt of gratitude to the

man who, by his wit, his courage,
and his industry, has brought about
reforms in our legal administration,
for which all litigants and honourable practitioners should alike be
grateful.

Sir CHARLES RUSSELL : Ladies
and gentlemen,—We have spent, I am
sure you will all think, a most enjoy-
able, as well as a most instructive evening, thanks to the vivid picture of the
great novelist of our generation put
before us by my friend Mr. Lockwood, who has pointed out with force
and effect the serious obligation we
are under for many reforms which
exist in our day through the influence,
sometimes serious, sometimes comic,
which the great Charles Dickens gave
to the world. It is an interesting
occasion, and not the less interesting when you are informed that in

this room to-night is the son of Mr.
Charles Dickens—Mr. Henry Fielding Dickens—referred to by my friend
Mr. Lockwood. Mr. Henry Dickens
has not followed in his father's footsteps ; he has chosen for himself the
profession of the bar ; and in that
profession he has gained for himself
a high and honourable name. At this
hour I cannot permit myself to say
more than to ask you to join in the
vote of thanks which I now move to
my friend Mr. Lockwood for the very
admirable lecture which he has just
given.

Vote of thanks seconded by MR.
HILLIARD.

Mr. HENRY FIELDING DICKENS :
Sir Charles Russell, ladies and gentlemen,—I assure you that when I came
into this room to-night I had no more
idea that I was to make any observa-

8

tions than—the man in the moon. I
came here with the idea of listening
to my old friend Mr. Frank Lockwood, with the sure and certain
knowledge that I should derive a
great deal of amusement and interest
from his lecture. In that I need
hardly say I have not been dis-
appointed ; but I assure you, ladies
and gentlemen, that I have not only
been interested, I have been touched.
I am not alluding to the very grace-
ful allusions and far too flattering
observation upon myself given by
the Attorney-General, but I am
alluding to the spirit pervading this
hall this evening—a spirit which
proves to me that the memory of my
father is still green among you all.
To us who have the honour of bearing his name, that memory, I need
hardly tell you, is still sacred ; and to

find that among his fellow-country-
men, though twenty-three years have
passed since his death, there is still
that feeling of affection felt for him
that was felt for him in his lifetime,
is most gratifying to us all. I assure
you with all the warmth in my heart,
and in the name of my sister and
other members of the family, that I
thank you most sincerely, not only for
your generous reception of myself,
but for the feeling you have demon-
strated that you bear for my dear
father.

Mr. FRANK LOCKWOOD: Sir
Charles Russell, ladies and gentlemen,—I shall only detain you to say
that I thank you for your great kindness to me to-night; it has been a
pleasure to me to come. I was to
have come, if I remember rightly, in
June or July, 1892 ; I could not come

because there was a General Election. I am very glad that I was not prevented from coming to-night by a— General Election.

THE END.

Hazell, Watson, & Viney, Ld., London and Aylesbury.